ROBERT C. MEHNER

THE
EXPERIENCE

Breaking through the Barriers
That Block Spiritual Growth

 Seedbed

Printed in the United States of America

Cover design by Strange Last Name
Page design by PerfecType, Nashville, Tennessee

Mehner, Robert C.
   The experience : breaking through the barriers that block spiritual growth / Robert C.
Mehner. – Franklin, Tennessee : Seedbed Publishing, ©2019.

   pages ; cm.

   Includes bibliographical references (pages 121-124).
   ISBN 9781628246698 (paperback : alk. paper)
   ISBN 9781628246704 (Mobi)
   ISBN 9781628246711 (ePub)
   ISBN 9781628246728 (uPDF)

   1. Spiritual formation. 2. Spiritual exercises. 3. Spiritual life--Christianity.
   I. Title.

BV4511.M43 2019   248   2019934195

SEEDBED PUBLISHING
Franklin, Tennessee
seedbed.com

For my loving wife, Kristy, and children, Stefan and Casey. Thank you for your love and support. And for my spiritual mentor for many years, Pastor Johnny Thomas. I miss you, my friend.

Contents

Foreword

I like timely books. Just having attended a New Room Conference in Brentwood, Tennessee, I so appreciated their emphasis there on bands. Rob Mehner has drafted a model for Christians around the world to capture the spirit of just what the band meeting is all about.

I have spent most of my life researching the life and theology of John Wesley. I am well aware of his emphasis on bands as the lifeblood of the movement called Methodism.

As you read, note especially Mehner's discussion of issues like unforgiveness and idolatry that propel the reader into his outlining the person and work of the Holy Spirit that enables the seeker to overcome. God does not promise to deliver us from trouble; God guarantees trouble that we might be at one with our neighbors and friends, many of whom have never heard an intelligent presentation of the gospel. Sixty percent of Americans cannot name the four Gospels. Significant here, however, is that Mehner demonstrates how the band can launch believers into the kind of body that can not only change them but also the world in which they live.

Christians are about gathering. Wesley insisted that there is no gospel but social gospel and no holiness but social holiness. Methodists that did not gather in small groups, sharing their faith and holding each other accountable, did not survive the onslaught of the eighteenth century. Mehner insists that Christians that do not gather, sharing their faith and holding each other accountable, will not survive the twenty-first century.

Rob Mehner has not only read the Bible, he has tested biblical principles on the mission field, both at home and abroad. Quite frankly, I trust the man. I like his balance between theory and praxis. I also appreciate his heart for the full gospel as it promises hope for those most in need of a Word from On High.

Read this book with interest and share it with your friends as an important way of sustaining your own walk and of reaching your neighbors for Jesus Christ.

Robert G. Tuttle Jr., PhD
Emeritus Professor of World Christianity
Asbury Seminary

Preface

Hunger is driven by two things. If I get a whiff or taste of my wife's chili, I become hungry for that chili. A positive interaction whets my appetite for more. Conversely, if I am deprived of food long enough (in my case, about an hour and a half), my hunger grows. In either case, there arises in me a desire to find food and eat it.

Spiritual hunger operates much the same way. Perhaps you've caught a glimpse of God's love and offer of abundant life and you absolutely want more. Or, maybe, life's circumstances have created a spiritual drought which has left you hopeless and powerless on your own. And, now, there is rising in you a desire for a deeper connection to God and to a story larger than your own little one.

In my experience there are two ingredients that work together to produce a strong, spiritual hunger. The first is active obedience. Perhaps you've had a small taste of God's love and purposes and you are thinking about doing this study because you want more. I would suggest God has put it in front of you for a reason and I encourage you to enter into it along with a few spiritual friends. The second ingredient is perseverance in adverse life situations. There is a rarely used word in our language that is found somewhat frequently in the Bible—*long-suffering*—which captures this idea.

Most of what you will find in this study was birthed during a season in my life when I was experiencing both of these things. The Holy Spirit had done a new work in me and I was experiencing the love, presence, and power of Jesus in my life like never before. At the same time, our family was living through problems of Goliathan proportions, and we felt completely knocked around, beaten up, and pushed down. With help from my coworker, Daniel Taylor, a class was formed from what God was revealing at that time. I taught and tweaked the class twice a year for the next ten-plus years. During that time, I saw God's power work through it to transform lives. With more than one thousand alumni, I've seen the following results:

- About 15 percent did not finish the class or completed it, saying, "Mmmm, not so great."
- About 70 percent were moved to follow up on one of the specific topics they recognized as critical to moving forward in their spiritual journey.

- About 15 percent saw significant life transformation; surrendering more of their lives to Jesus and becoming better spouses, parents, employees, friends, and ambassadors for God's kingdom.
- Some who were in the first or second categories moved to the second or third after they repeated the class with a friend.

One more set of bullet points before I close. While I sincerely and completely give God all the glory for any life change experienced by another person, I believe there are factors which God uses or even helps orchestrate to increase the impact of the class, and this study in daily devotional form:

- The level of hunger that a participant has at the time of doing the study; whether driven by a taste of God's goodness or a season in the desert.
- The level of commitment to do the work and pray "show me" prayers daily. For example, "God, show me the obstacles preventing me from drawing nearer to you, being more effecive in my witness to you, loving and serving those around me, and becoming the person you created me to be."

- The presence of a small group participating together to support and pray for one another, and to reinforce what God is doing in each one of them.

Are you hungry? Are you searching for something to satisfy that hunger? Then dive right in with a few of your spiritual friends and see what God will do.

Note: I have facilitated the actual class in a two- to three-day retreat format for church staffs and leadership groups. Contact me if you would like to explore that option for your organization.

Acknowledgments

This work is born out of a class called The Experience, which I taught for more than ten years at La Croix Church in Cape Girardeau, Missouri. I am grateful for their support and for the feedback from those who participated in the class. I am also grateful to Pastor Daniel Taylor and Chris Patterson for their input to the class.

What Are You Seeking? and Four Other Big Questions about Our Spiritual Journeys

Day 1
What Are You Seeking?
Isaiah 57:14–15; 61:1–3; John 1:35–37

Imagine a dog in an open field hooked to a long leash that is tethered to a post hammered deep into the ground. The dog can walk or run until it reaches the end of its rope. Then if it continues to run and pull harder to move forward, it exhausts itself by running in circles and digging deeper and deeper ruts. Our spiritual journeys often look much like this.

As a pastor for twenty years I have focused on spiritual health and growth. I have a passion to see people become all God created them to be. In those twenty years,

I've enjoyed nothing more than helping people experience the things we read in Isaiah 61:

- knowledge of the good news of Jesus Christ and the love of God;
- healing of a broken heart;
- freedom and light;
- comfort, joy, passion, and empowerment;
- being grounded yet knowing adventure;
- salvation and right relationships (with God and others); and
- restoration and justice.

This is what Jesus said he came to give us, but so many are living a tethered, exhausting existence.

We grow and move forward, sometimes with great speed, and then—BAM!—something chokes us and keeps us stuck in one spot. The typical advice from church leaders or spiritual friends is to read the Bible more, pray more, or go to more church activities and events. But, typically, this leads to fatigue and frustration from running in circles and digging ruts in our spiritual lives with no forward movement. Then we just sit down and settle for something far less than the abundant life Jesus told us he came to give us.

Jesus asked two of his disciples just as they began following him, "What are you seeking?" (John 1:38). He asks each of us as well. Do you want to grow spiritually and experience more of the abundant life God has purposed for you? If so, then this study will help you overcome common obstacles that prevent us from experiencing healing, joy, spiritual maturity, and divine power to impact the world for Jesus Christ.

Closing Exercise

Commit to spending the time necessary to allow God to work through this study. Take ten minutes or less to read the daily Scriptures and devotional. Then devote a couple of five-minute periods during your day to pray contemplatively or to complete the short exercise. Finally, commit to sharing with your group or a spiritual friend what God is doing in you through this study.

—————— **Day 2** ——————
A Journey Led by God
Luke 5:1–11

There are many people who have no real idea what is meant by discipleship or spiritual formation. Others reduce the meaning to religious practices like prayer, corporate worship, and reading the Bible. While such practices are important tools in our discipleship and spiritual maturity, they are not in and of themselves discipleship nor spiritual formation.

So, what are discipleship and spiritual formation? They are different terms for the same lifelong process of deepening our relationship with God in a way that transforms us. To deepen a relationship requires growing in understanding of ourselves, others, and of our interactions. Spiritual formation is about learning who God is, who we are, and what we are to become; how we are to relate to God and others. Spiritual disciplines definitely help. Reading the Bible reveals exactly these things. Praying connects us to the Holy Spirit who guides and empowers us. Corporate worship connects us to other followers of Jesus in God's presence.

But spiritual practices are not enough. To be a disciple of Jesus Christ means to submit our small story to God's larger story, to have our lives serve God's purposes rather than our own. I don't recall who said it, but I love this quote: "God is always inviting us to play a small role in the greatest film ever made, but we regularly demand to be the star in a B movie no one will ever remember." A grand purpose of our spiritual formation is to realize our full potential in serving God and his kingdom. And God is the leader in that process.

Read through the book of Luke and watch Jesus disciple his disciples. He reveals who he and the Father really are. He prods the disciples out of their small stories and into the Father's greater story. At each point, there is a critical decision to be made. Will Peter the fisherman let a carpenter tell him how to fish? How will the disciples respond to Jesus' comfort with their discomfort during a life-threatening storm? Will they forfeit their traditional ways of interacting with God in order to find the intimacy Jesus has with his Father? Will they accept the cost of following Jesus when the reward is for the lost rather than them? Will they continue to follow Jesus through amazing mountaintops and dark valleys that threaten their very lives? Will they remain in spiritually forming community (as the Twelve) despite their differences and disagreements?

While the context of our spiritual formation is different, Jesus presents the same basic opportunities and questions to us. Will we submit our small stories to God's greater story, follow Jesus where he leads, and do so in authentic community?

Closing Exercise

Identify where God is saying to you as he did to Peter in Luke 5, "Put out a little further . . . come follow me." Ask him to help you respond, "Because you say so, I will do it."

Throughout this study we will engage in "show me" prayers, asking God to reveal certain things to us. If this is a new concept of asking for God to speak and then listening for the Holy Spirit, try the following exercise. Close your eyes and imagine yourself in your favorite place (beach, mountains, wherever) on a perfect day. As you relax and enjoy this time, imagine Jesus is now sitting next to you, simply enjoying what you are enjoying. Imagine this for two to five minutes. Then without speaking, ask Jesus what he would like to say. How does he respond? Share the result of this exercise with your group.

Day 3
Where Are You?
Colossians 1:9–10; Hebrews 6:1–3

If you are standing in front of a large directory map at a mall, you must locate two things for the directory to be helpful: the "You Are Here" indicator and the store you'd like to visit. This is true for our spiritual journeys as well. We must know where we are (today's focus) and where we are going (tomorrow's focus). There are any number of tools that can help locate you on the discipleship map. One church uses a line from -10 to 10, where -10 is actively killing Christians, 0 is accepting Jesus, and 10 is like Mother Teresa on steroids. Some churches use categories such as Exploring Christ, Growing in Christ, Close to Christ, and Christ-Centered.

The accompanying question to "Where are you?" is "Why are you there?" If you are passing through a point or category as a normal part of your spiritual formation, that's great! But if you are stuck there or have returned there, not so great. Imagine you are on a trip from one side of the United States to the other. If you find yourself in St. Louis because it's a point on the way, then there is no problem. If you find yourself in St. Louis for the third time on your journey, it's a problem. If floodwaters cover the Mississippi River bridge, that's an obstacle, but if you've run out of gas, that's a process problem. Sometimes we get stuck in our spiritual journeys due to obstacles. (We will spend much of our time in the coming weeks looking at three very common obstacles.) But sometimes we get stuck due to process problems. I will share three of those with you today.

First, the spiritual activities that catalyze our movement from one category to the next change as we grow.

Second, our growth is typically rapid early in the journey and heavily reliant on church programs. We grow fast early on by showing up and participating in things others have initiated. However, along the way our growth becomes slower and the responsibility shifts to ours. We often remember the early growth, romanticize the activities associated with it, and never want to move on to new activities. We begin to complain that church services, small groups, and leadership just aren't what they used to be. In reality, the issue is that we have grown and what we need to continue forward has changed. Our refusal to move from comfortable but ineffective practices and activities has us stuck. Are we willing to leave behind our boats and nets in order to follow Jesus further on the journey?

Third, the spiritual journey is a communal journey. While we need times of solitude along the way, the journey demands spiritual friends, mentors, and mentees to help us find our way forward. If we want to do this journey alone, we're precisely who God wants to place in a community.

Closing Exercise

Ask God to show you any spiritual activity or practice in which you are engaged that is no longer catalyzing your growth. Also ask him to show you a catalytic one that might replace it. Share your thoughts with your group members.

Day 4
Where Are You Going and Do You Want to Get There?

Romans 8:29; Galatians 5:22–25; Matthew 16:24–26; John 5:3–6; Mark 10:17–22

Of the four big questions, "Where are you going?" is the easiest because the answer has been given to us. The Christian spiritual journey has Christlikeness as its destination. Romans 8:29 says that the outcome God has always had in mind for us is to be like Jesus. What does that look like? Galatians 5:22–23 tells us that over time we will consistently become more loving, joyful, peaceful, patient and long-suffering, kind, good, faithful, gentle, and self-controlled. These things are called "fruit of the Spirit," which means they naturally blossom in our lives when we are moving forward with the Holy Spirit toward Christlikeness. If we do not see a measure of increase in at least some of these fruits, then we are probably stuck in our spiritual journey or traveling to somewhere other than Christlikeness.

Notice that these indicators of forward movement toward Christlikeness are not called "fruit of _____ (fill in your name)" nor "fruit of my church/pastor." Trying to manage our behaviors in order to be more loving, kind, patient, et cetera, is exhausting. And while being influenced by the lives of mature Christians is helpful, relying on another human being to produce fruit in our lives is a dead end. Only God's work in us through the Holy Spirit can consistently and successfully cultivate these Christlike character traits in our lives. The Holy Spirit leads, but we must cooperate, and that's where our third big question comes into play: Do I want to go to Christlikeness?

This might seem like a silly question, but no sillier than Jesus asking a paralytic, "Do you want to be healed?" (John 5:6). People generally give three answers to this question:

1. *Yes.* If this is your answer you are ready to move forward.
2. *No.* An answer not reserved for nonbelievers. Perhaps you, like many in the church, consider Christlikeness to be extreme, fanatical, and reserved for clergy and super-Jesus-freaks.

3. *I wish I was Christlike*. The more common answer among believers is the third answer. But there is a huge difference between wanting something and wishing it were so. If we wish to be Christlike, we're asking God to wave a wand and make it so without our effort and hopefully without too much disruption to our lives.

A wished-for journey toward Christlikeness stops when things get hard or uncomfortable. The rich young ruler in Mark 10 wished for heaven, but didn't want it badly enough to cut loose the idol that had his heart. I had personally lived many years wishing for Christlikeness without really *wanting* to go badly enough to do what was necessary: to deny my own life and take up my cross daily.

Closing Exercise

Discuss the following questions with your group: (1) Have you seen growth in any aspect of the fruit of the Spirit in the last year? Explain. (2) Have you left something behind in the last three to five years to follow Jesus more fully? (3) Are you willing to give something up now to move forward?

———— Day 5 ————
What Obstacles Are in Your Way?
Isaiah 57:14–15; John 16:33; Psalm 23

Recall the tethered dog metaphor from Day 1 and how it can represent our stationary spiritual journeys. Running and digging harder will not help the dog move forward, nor will overindulging in religious practices help us when we become stuck. What is needed is to step back, loosen the tension, identify what has us stuck, and allow God to remove the obstacle standing in the way.

We should not be surprised that we encounter obstacles on our spiritual journey. We are broken individuals living among broken people in a broken world. As we read about the spiritual journeys of the disciples, we will discover the obstacles and hiccups they faced. Also, we should not condemn ourselves when we are tripped up by obstacles. Shame and self-condemnation only increase and fortify our obstacles. Learning from our stumbles and taking time to allow God's Spirit to lead us in overcoming them is the way forward.

Over the next few weeks we will identify and discuss three very common obstacles that halt our spiritual journeys. While there can be any number of obstacles in all sizes, these three have been the most prevalent in my twenty years of work in spiritual direction, pastoral care, and counseling. They are:

- the refusal or inability to forgive;
- our past wounds and how the enemy of our souls uses them to have us living out of lies; and
- idolatry, religion, and habitual sin.

And, of course, we will learn together what helps us overcome these obstacles and move forward toward Christlikeness.

Closing Exercise

Ask God to show you over the next several weeks what obstacles are in your way. Do not jump into trying to overcome them right away since we will talk more about that process. Share with your group if God reveals anything to you, or share which of the obstacles most interests or concerns you.

The Obstacle of Unforgiveness

Day 1
Overview
Matthew 6:14–15; Luke 6:37

Throughout my many years as a spiritual formation pastor and spiritual guide, I have found the most frequent obstacle preventing forward movement in a person's spiritual journey is unforgiveness. (By the way, I just learned "unforgiveness" is not a word; that the negative noun form of forgive is "unforgivingness." I think I'll stick to "unforgiveness.") It may not be the most difficult obstacle to overcome, but it is one of the most common. This is true for a combination of three reasons:

- the frequency with which broken people mistreat us and require our forgiveness;

- the common misunderstandings people have about what forgiveness is and is not; and
- the reality that people rarely forgive completely; usually finding a way to forgive the other person for their actions but not for the resulting pain and consequences that their actions have brought to their lives.

Yet the Bible consistently calls for us to forgive one another. Our Scripture readings for today are just an example; there are others that appear even more emphatic. Jesus tells a parable about forgiveness to Peter in the eighteenth chapter of Matthew which we will return to later this week, but for now I'll simply share the unsettling ending to the story about a person forgiven who refused to forgive another for a smaller offense.

> "Then the king called in the man he had forgiven and said, 'You evil servant! I forgave you that tremendous debt because you pleaded with me. Shouldn't you have mercy on your fellow servant, just as I had mercy on you?' Then the angry king sent the man to prison to be tortured until he had paid his entire debt.
>
> "That's what my heavenly Father will do to you if you refuse to forgive your brothers and sisters from your heart." (Matt. 18:32–35 NLT)

It's not that God is lurking over us, waiting to hammer us if we get this forgiveness thing wrong. It's that he knows rather than our receiving the abundant life and transformation into Christlikeness that he so desires for us, we will experience the imprisonment and torture of bitterness if we fail to forgive as he has forgiven us.

Closing Exercise

Pray the "show-me" prayer: "Lord, show me if there is any unforgiveness in me. Show me who I need to forgive so that I might be free to experience your transforming grace and mercy in my life. Help me to trust that you can empower me to forgive beyond what I've been able to do so far. Use the next several days of this study to increase my capacity to forgive. Amen."

Day 2
What Forgiveness Is Not
Psalm 1:1; Proverbs 26:11

To clearly understand forgiveness, it is helpful to begin with what it is not. Forgiveness is not:

- saying that what someone did to us is really okay (excusing);

- saying that what someone did to us is not that big of a deal or is understandable given their circumstances (minimizing);
- a one-time thing; rather it is a process that takes time and repetition as life retriggers known hurts or reveals those we were unaware existed;
- trusting the offender once again; or
- reconciling with the offender.

In the following days, we will see how excusing or minimizing the offense against us actually prevents us from forgiving, and why forgiveness is not like an on-off switch; either we have or have not forgiven someone. Today, we will address the issues of trust and reconciliation.

I have heard smart, good, well-intentioned people teach that forgiveness *requires* reconciliation and trust. I wholeheartedly disagree. It's a blessing when forgiveness leads to reconciliation and trust, but those are secondary steps which follow forgiveness. Trust and reconciliation require participation by both people, offended and offender. Forgiveness requires only the action of the offended person (though it may include both). You can forgive an untrustworthy, destructive person without trusting them or entering back into relationship with them. This is good news since you should not trust them nor reconcile if they are untrustworthy and destructive. You don't need to be there when the dog returns to its vomit! (see Proverbs 26:11). But you can forgive while maintaining appropriate boundaries. Many people with whom I've worked have found the freedom to forgive once they understood that trust and reconciliation are independent steps that may or may not occur after the primary step of forgiveness.

Closing Exercise

Continue to ask God this week to show you if there is any forgiving for you to do. Share with your group the results of this prayer and pray for one another that God will help you forgive. Also share your thoughts about the difference between forgiveness, trust, and reconciliation.

—————— **Day 3** ——————
What Forgiveness Is
Matthew 5:7; Luke 6:36

Yesterday we saw that forgiveness is not reestablishing trust or reconciling with another person, nor is it a one-time event but rather a process. Today we will use a familiar metaphor to illustrate that excusing or minimizing what someone has done prevents us from forgiving them.

When a person hurts us, it is very much like they write us a legally binding IOU for the cost of their sin. Many people collect IOUs, holding them up in front of their faces, looking at their entire world through the IOUs. All of life becomes associated with how they've been wronged, causing them to project anger and disappointment onto others who had nothing to do with the offense. They are often seen as wounded malcontents. Others stuff the IOUs into their pockets and pretend they weren't hurt. The weight of these hidden debts makes them emotionally distant. Obsessing over and hiding IOUs are common responses, but not healthy ones.

Forgiveness occurs when we closely examine the IOU, paying special attention to its value, being honest with ourselves about how our heart, mind, and ability to relate to others has been impacted and assessing all the ways we've been affected. Once we deeply understand the value of the IOU, we then choose to tear it up, nullifying what is owed to us, cancelling the debt. The only time an accounts receivable department writes off an IOU is when they are convinced it can never be repaid. It's critical to understand that a person who sins against us and owes us better can *never* repay the debt. That person may be nice to us the rest of our lives and ask for forgiveness, but he or she cannot go back and undo what was done or repair the hurt. So we are bound to that person, that offense, that wound, and that unpaid IOU until we choose to tear it up.

And the entire amount must be pardoned. Minimizing or excusing what was done causes us to cancel only a portion of the debt. We must be aware and honest with ourselves about what is owed, which requires courage to enter back into our pain, to name the offense and hurt, and to evaluate what was taken and inflicted. With mild offenses, this may happen quickly and without conscious thought. But greater offenses require intention and diligence; one reason why forgiveness is a process. Often people tell me, "I thought I forgave that person, but now I'm not sure." You may have forgiven someone for the full value of the IOU as you understood it at the time, but later discover additional injury that must be forgiven or something happens to trigger the old hurts and you need to forgive again for the fresh pain you're experiencing.

Closing Exercise

Ask God to show you if there is someone you need to more fully forgive. If appropriate, share with your group anything God reveals and ask them to pray with you for God to give you strength to forgive.

———— Day 4 ————
How Forgiving Others
Impacts Your Forgiveness
Matthew 18:21–35

Imagine you are holding a cup in your left hand, centered above a large bowl. Now imagine a huge pitcher pouring water into the cup until it overflows into the bowl. The cup represents your life, the bowl is the world around you, and the water from the pitcher is the love and mercy (forgiveness) from God pouring into your life. It fills the cup to overflowing so that what naturally happens is love and forgiveness flow out of you to the world around you.

Now, imagine that you don't want to forgive someone in the world around you. How do you stop the overflow of love and mercy spilling on the world around you? No matter where you move the cup, the bowl moves with you (there is always a world around you). The only option is to put your right hand over the top of the cup. This stops the overflow from your cup.

Now consider the parable from today's Bible reading. It is easy to think this parable is saying that when I put my hand over my cup and refuse to forgive, God angrily walks away with his pitcher of love and mercy while saying, "Well, if you won't forgive then I don't like you anymore and I'm taking my pitcher and going home." But we know that's not our compassionate heavenly Father's character. To understand what the parable means, we need to now imagine that there is a hole in the bottom of the cup. We are not perfect; we desperately need God's love and mercy because we leak! With our hands over the top, our cups soon become empty (ironically, while God's love and mercy still runs off our hands and onto the world around us). Do you know what an empty-cup kind of life looks like? I do, because I've seen it time and again. It looks like angry, bitter, isolated, and old before one's time.

While God's love and mercy flow continuously, it is possible to put ourselves in a position that prevents us from receiving it. Over time, this leads to an empty life of unresolved anger, then bitterness, and finally isolation. It is a life of "weeping and gnashing of teeth" (see Matthew 8:12; 13:42; 22:13; 24:51; 25:30), a living hell. As one of my mentors Dr. Robert Tuttle says, "You don't have to die to experience hell."

A common question after this lesson is: What if the person I'm struggling to forgive is me? We will address that question toward the end of next week.

Closing Exercise

Ask God to show you if any unforgiveness is interfering with his flow of love and mercy into your life. If appropriate, share with your group anything God reveals. Pray together, asking God to fill you to overflowing again with his love and mercy.

————— **Day 5** —————

The Effect of Forgiveness on Love

Luke 7:36–50; Isaiah 53:4–5

At the end of the encounter in Luke 7, Jesus makes a direct connection between forgiveness and love. Those who are forgiven much, love much and those who are forgiven little, love little (v. 47). Jesus is not saying that people who have sinned more in their lives are better equipped to love; rather, Jesus is communicating to the Pharisee that he needed forgiveness like we all need forgiveness. If we view ourselves as righteous or less in need of a Savior and his grace than those around us, then we love God less, love other people less, and judge them more.

On the cross, Jesus took on himself our guilt and sentence for the sins we have committed. But what is also true is that Jesus took on all the pain and suffering that has resulted from sin. In my work with those who have endured physical and sexual abuse as children, this is an incredibly important point that makes the cross more than just something for those who abused them. It answers the question: Where was God when this happened to me? And the answer is that he was hanging on a cross taking into his own body, mind, and heart all of your experience, so that for all eternity there will be only two people who know what it was like for you to endure what you have endured—you and Jesus. "Surely he took up our pain and bore our suffering . . . and by his wounds we are healed" (Isa. 53:4–5 NIV). God, for all eternity, will use something evil which he never desired for us to bring us closer to him. How he did this is surely a mystery, as is how he took on the guilt and sentence of all sin; but it is just as true.

Therefore, Jesus offers forgiveness to the person who has sinned against us not from a position of ignorance, but from the position of having experienced what we have experienced. Jesus is not asking us to do anything he has not already done. Nor is he asking us to offer anything he has not already offered to us. Romans 5:8 says, "But God demonstrates his own love for us in this: While we were still sinners, Christ died for us" (NIV). Again, God's Word connects love and forgiveness. When he asks us to forgive, he knows that it will reconcile us to him, to others, and to ourselves in a way that heals us and increases our capacity to love. It is his love for us and his desire for our healing that is behind his command for us to forgive as he has forgiven. It is another way in which he calls to us, "Take up [your] cross and follow me" (Matt. 16:24).

Closing Exercise

One exercise that many people have found helpful in forgiving someone, particularly someone who has died, is to write a letter to the person you need to forgive. You will not send the letter, so do not filter your sadness, frustration, anger, or rage. Write until you can write no more, then put it away for a few weeks before returning to read it. If necessary, write more or clarify what you've written. When finished, you can either destroy it or ask one of your group members to stand in the place of the person who wronged you, read the letter to him or her, and have that person ask for your forgiveness. When you are ready, destroy the letter and express out loud your decision to forgive.

The Obstacle of Our Past, Our Enemy, and Living with Lies

Day 1
Beliefs vs. Convictions: Part 1
Proverbs 14:10; 1 John 3:19–21

We all walk through life with beliefs and convictions (things of which we are convinced). Beliefs are formed in our brains by a logical process of considering a truth statement and accepting, rejecting, or modifying it. We also have beliefs from indoctrination (especially by our family of origin). Beliefs are formed and reside in our brains and collectively they form our conscious worldview. We *speak* out of our beliefs and we really mean it. Convictions, or things we are convinced of, are formed by our experiences and interpretation of those experiences. They reside in the emotional center of our being, provide the foundation for our subconscious worldview, and greatly impact how we see ourselves, others, and God. We *behave* out of our convictions as they produce our coping mechanisms—both offensive and defensive.

Some of our beliefs and convictions are misaligned or diametrically opposed to one another. This is why we sometimes behave counter to what we profess. A person with incongruent beliefs and convictions experiences inner turmoil—an internal civil war of sorts. We often respond to situations in the same unhealthy or destructive ways even though we *know* (believe) it is wrong. Both beliefs and convictions can be right or wrong, but it is false convictions, or lies we've bought into, that most often stunt our spiritual growth. While it is not always the case, convictions are typically formed by painful events.

We are all wounded in life, some in small ways and others in unbelievably tragic ways. As we do our best to survive and recover from the hurt, we also interpret these events. We ask, "Why did this happen and what does it say about me, about others, and about God?" Particularly when we are young, we struggle to interpret these events correctly because our brains are not fully developed and we are "me" centric—certain that everything happened *at* me or *because of* me. This is why you cannot convince a seven-year-old that she's not the reason her parents just divorced. Even if she *believes* what you are telling her, she's *convinced* otherwise.

In our pain we misinterpret an event, often with the help of our lying enemy (we will learn more about this over the next two days), and we become convinced of something that seems true but isn't. Then these convictions produce behaviors in us that cause those around us to react in ways that support the original lie. I'll give an example of this in the coming days, but let me say it once again: our false convictions drive behaviors in us that cause the people around us to respond in ways that make us even more certain of our false conviction.

Closing Exercise

We will return to this topic in a few days, but begin to ask God to show you if you are convinced of anything that is not true and that is causing you to behave contrary to your beliefs or God's freeing and healing truth.

─────── **Day 2** ───────
Our Enemy, Part 1: Who He Is
John 12:27–31, 14:28–31, 16:7–11;
Genesis 1:26–28; Luke 4:5–8

A key component of our developing false convictions is the work of our spiritual enemy, Satan. There are two schools of thought on opposite ends of the spectrum about the topic of personified evil (Satan) and neither is helpful. The first says that Satan was derived by ignorant people steeped in mythology, and that anyone believing such a thing is superstitious or uneducated. The second is the certainty that Satan and his minions are responsible for anything remotely negative that happens; if I sneeze it's because a demon ran up my nose and not because of the dust I inhaled. I have found that the topic of Satan causes people to put their heads in the sand, but this is exactly what the Bible tells us *not* to do.

We know that Scripture supports the existence of the devil and demons because of the encounters Jesus has with them. But beyond mere existence, the Bible gives us a good picture of who Satan is, why he has power to act here on earth, and how he typically works. In John's Gospel chapters 12, 14, and 16, Jesus refers to Satan as "the prince of this world." A prince is given authority by the king to rule in a geographical region within his kingdom. Hence, a prince has real power and authority, though not ultimate power and authority. It's kind of like a franchise. The owner of your local Burger King has real authority within that restaurant to hire and fire and manage affairs, but the local Burger King owner does not have authority over the entire entity called Burger King.

Jesus is saying that Satan has real power and authority on earth. But why would God give Satan that kind of power in his creation? He didn't. We read in Genesis 1:26–28 that God gave dominion to humankind. When we rebelled against God, we inadvertently handed our God-given authority over to Satan. Jesus reinforces this in Luke 4:6–7 when he does not challenge Satan's claim, "I will give you all the authority and splendor [of the kingdoms of this world]; it has been given to me, and I can give it to anyone I want to. If you worship me, it will all be yours" (NIV). He simply responds, "It is written: 'Worship the Lord your God and serve him only'" (v. 8 NIV).

God meant it when he said humankind had dominion, rule, and reign in this world. He was serious enough to endure the mess we've made of his creation; serious enough to suffer and die to provide for its redemption; serious enough to allow the consequence of his enemy having authority and power in his own creation, if only for a time until he fully restores his kingdom here on earth.

Closing Exercise

Continue to ask God to show you if you are convinced of anything that is not true and that is causing you to behave contrary to your beliefs or fully live in God's truth. Ask God to solidify his truth from 1 John 4:4: "You, dear children, are from God and have overcome them, because the one who is in you is greater than the one who is in the world."

————————— **Day 3** —————————

Our Enemy, Part 2: How He Works
1 Peter 5:8; Ephesians 6:10–20;
Revelation 12:10; John 8:43–44

Today, let's look at *how* Satan works with the power and authority he has co-opted from us. Again, we turn to the Scriptures listed for today. In 1 Peter 5:8 we find that Satan "prowls around like a roaring lion looking for someone to devour." Most of us have seen a video of lions hunting and know that they pursue the weak, the sick, the young, and the isolated. This is what Peter is communicating; Satan looks to pounce on the vulnerable. Ephesians 6 says he has schemes and shoots fiery arrows (not literally, stay with me and we'll understand these momentarily). In Revelation 12 we see that Satan is constantly accusing us about our shortcomings and sin. That's a scheme if I ever saw one! Finally, in John 8, we see that Satan lies, lies, and lies some more! Lies are the main type of fiery arrow that Satan uses; they lodge in one's heart as false convictions.

Specifically, here is how Satan helps produce false convictions in our lives. He comes in our most vulnerable moments and tells us lies—really good lies. A bad lie is 180 degrees from the truth and, therefore, is easy to detect and simple to defuse. Good lies are 3 degrees off the truth and sound very much like the truth because they contain a great deal of it. So he sidles up beside us in our pain, whispers a good lie in our ears, and we become *convinced* that it is true. A false conviction in the emotional center of our being is formed and it drives behaviors that make others react in a way to affirm the lie over and over again. Slowly our lives fall further and further short of the free and abundant life God intended for us.

Or, rather than suffering, we have success. Things go really well for us in school, sports, music, art, work, or outward beauty. We can quickly find ourselves overconfident in our own strength and ability, which leaves us isolated with a false identity built around achievement—we are what we accomplish. In these instances, the enemy of our soul whispers, "Well, well, well, look at you. Aren't you something?! Why, someone like you doesn't need anything or anybody. You are quite capable of doing it your way, when you want, and how you want to do it." The self-reliant man or woman is set up for the rug to be pulled out from under them later on—when a loved one dies, or divorce comes, or the inability to have children is diagnosed, or the pink slip shows up, or the child rebels. However and whenever the rug is pulled, the fall is hard.

Closing Exercise

Continue to ask God to show you if you are convinced of anything that is not true and that is causing you to behave contrary to your beliefs or not fully live in God's truth. Specifically, ask God if you are living out of pride or overconfidence in a way that leaves you vulnerable and isolated to the schemes of Satan.

——— Day 4 ———
Beliefs vs. Convictions: Part 2
John 16:13; 2 Corinthians 10:5

Today I want to share a story from my life that serves as a good, though mild example of false convictions, and how believing these lies caused others to react to me in ways that made me believe the lies even more.

I grew up with three older siblings—two sisters, ten and eight years older, and a brother six years older. We were very close and spent a great deal of time together. My relationship with my siblings shaped my identity; it's how I understood who I was and what role I played. In a little over a year, when I was twelve years old, both my sisters married and my brother moved away to attend college. I experienced agonizing loneliness and identity disorientation. While none of my siblings had done anything wrong nor intended to hurt me, I was hurt nonetheless.

There I was, wounded and confused, isolated and lonely. Here he came—the prince of this world—with two murderous lies. The first one was, "No matter how much people act like they love you, they will leave you and hurt you!" The second was, "You thought you were so likeable; better try a lot harder!" You can see the quality of the lies. There will be times when people who love me will leave, but not because they were pretending or there is something inherently wrong with me. Some people will not like me, but not because I'm unlikeable or need to earn their approval or affection.

When I bought into those two lies it produced some specific behaviors. As I got older, some people approached me because they were interested in knowing me better or having a relationship of some kind. When they did, the first lie would kick in and, to protect myself, I would be very guarded. (Imagine me stiff-arming these people to keep them at a distance.) Or I would meet someone that I thought was interesting, whom I would like to get to know better, and the second lie would kick in. So I would try way too hard to get those people to like me. Of course, when I stiff-armed people, they left. And when they left, I thought, "See, I knew it; these people who pretend to like me leave me!" Lie number 1 affirmed and solidified. And when I tried way too hard to get others to like me, they rejected me. Then I would hear in my heart, "Still not good enough . . . better try harder next time!" Lie number 2 affirmed and solidified. *Believing lies creates behavior that solicits reactions that affirm the lie.*

Actually, I was confident; I *believed* I was likeable and I *believed* people wanted to be friends with me and not leave me. But I was *convinced* otherwise. What to do? Tomorrow . . .

Closing Exercise

Ask God to show you specific, recurring behaviors in your life which are born out of wounds and lies. If appropriate, discuss these among your group and pray for one another to receive healing and truth.

——————— **Day 5** ———————

Truth, Freedom, and Forgiving Ourselves
Psalm 51:1–12; Romans 8:26–28

Jesus said, "You will know the truth, and the truth will set you free" (John 8:32). Do we want to be free? Do we *want* to be free or do we just wish we were free? If we want to be free we will have to deal with these flaming arrows from the enemy of our souls—the lies and false convictions that drive so many of the destructive behaviors we use to cope (alcohol, drugs, porn, etc.). But how?

First, remember that God is more powerful than our enemy (1 John 4:4). God's Spirit of Truth is available to shed light on the dark spots in our hearts. King David knew this. He wrote Psalm 51 after committing adultery and conspiring to commit murder. "You [God] desire truth in the innermost being, and in the hidden part You will make me know wisdom" (v. 6 NASB). David is saying, "I *believe* you are a forgiving God and can cleanse me, but I need to be *convinced* of it in the deepest and darkest parts of my heart." We need the same thing to happen in our hearts. Second, we need to be aware of behaviors that we *know* aren't right but consistently do when triggered in certain ways. It could be being cut off in traffic, criticized or blamed, or some other event, small or large. Often these are signals of behavior based in false convictions. Finally, we must allow God to fully heal the wounds associated with the false convictions we discover. It's what Jesus came to do—bind the brokenhearted and set the captives free!

This sounds easy, but often people won't allow God to do it. This is because it typically involves letting God take us back into the pain or events that produced the false convictions. This isn't easy nor is it for the fainthearted. My dad had one go-to cure for cuts and abrasions: rubbing alcohol. While it was effective at cleaning out a wound and preventing infection, it *really hurt*! So my brother and I would hide our injuries, sometimes resulting in a scabbed-over wound with infection underneath. When these were discovered, my dad would scrub the wound open with a rough rag and then pour alcohol on it. I want you to know up front that the path to God's healing of old wounds is often similarly painful and sometimes about as gruesome. But the health and freedom we experience is worth the pain. God sometimes has to let us hurt in order to save us from harm and to restore us to the people he created us to be.

Often this process involves forgiving others or ourselves. This is not easy, but we cannot be legalistic or pharisaical with one another or ourselves. Rather, we must recognize our need for forgiveness and find our way to Jesus, like the sinful woman in Luke 7, using the same principles of forgiveness that we explored last week. Then we can agree with Jesus, who says we are already forgiven!

Closing Exercise

Pray that God would make you aware of behaviors driven by false convictions. Ask him to reveal and plant in your heart his truth that will overcome these false convictions. Pray that, if necessary, he reveals the wounds that led to the false conviction, and that he heals/transforms you.

The Obstacle of Idolatry

Day 1
How the Mind Really Works
(According to Romans 8)

Romans 8:5–8 (read in NIV, NLT, and CEB);
Matthew 7:13–14

We like to think that our minds are completely free in every way to make whatever decision we want. But according to Romans 8:5–8 our minds operate much more like computer central processing units (CPUs). Given certain inputs, a CPU is designed to give predictable outputs. Give the input of flesh, self, world, or sin (depending on your translation), and the mind will make decisions and choices that lead to a specific outcome: *death.* Given inputs from the Holy Spirit, the mind will make decisions and choices that lead to a different outcome: *life and peace*. Dallas Willard summarizes by saying that there are two options:

- the body controls the mind, negatively impacting our spirit, leading to spiritual death; or
- the Holy Spirit controls the mind and impacts behavior, leading to life and peace.

If we believe this to be true, the question becomes: Why would anyone willingly allow inputs into his or her brain that lead to death rather than inputs that lead to life and peace? The answers are actually straightforward.

First, the inputs of flesh, self, and sin are loud and prevelant. There are very few places one can escape from the worldly messages of . . . well . . . the world. They are screamed in our ear constantly without any effort or intention on our part. The inputs of the Spirit are quiet and require us to be intentional in order to hear or notice them.

Second, while the inputs of flesh, self, and sin eventually lead to death, the road that leads to that death feels great, is all about us, makes us look important or cool, and is culturally normal. The inputs of the Spirit are just the opposite. It's true that life and peace await us further down the road, but the way is often difficult, self-sacrificial, and culturally weird. Matthew 7:13–14 confirms this.

Tomorrow we will move to the topic of idols, but first let's introduce a workable definition of "idol." An idol, in the spiritual rather than pop culture sense, is that which our mind is *most* fixed on. There may be many inputs into our minds, but the one that trumps the others is our idol.

Closing Exercise

Reflect on the inputs that are commonly entering your mind. Think about their sources and how these inputs impact your life. How often are inputs of world, self, and sin entering your mind versus inputs of the Holy Spirit? Share your thoughts with your group.

Day 2

The Three Two-Faced Idols

Matthew 16:21–25; Exodus 20:1–3

In *The Importance of Being Foolish*, author Brennan Manning identifies three idols and says all other idols fall under these three. I agree with him with a slight addition I'll mention which I find helps people better identify where they may struggle with idolatry. I'll make a major alteration tomorrow. The slight addition is to think of the three idols as being two-faced, like coins with heads and tails. They are:

- seeking security (heads) or escaping insecurity (tails);
- seeking power or control (heads) or escaping commitment, fear, or insignificance (tails); and
- seeking pleasure (heads) or escaping pain or numbness (tails).

Idolatry is desiring these things more than we desire God. And remember that when our minds are set on security, control, and pleasure, it leads to death, according to Romans 8. "Death of what?" you may ask. Good question.

Chasing after security or escaping insecurity kills intimacy by eliminating vulnerability, honesty, trust, and transparency. We cannot strive for security while trusting others and being vulnerable. Those things are opposed to one another. But without transparency and trust, we cannot be fully intimate with one another, so our relationships suffer.

Chasing power and control or escaping commitment, fear, or insignificance kills love because it requires us to objectify those around us (whether we are aware of it or not). We cannot manipulate and sacrifice people like pawns on a chessboard if we don't first objectify them, and we can't love objects though we may love what objects do *for* us. People and relationships become means to an end, so lust and envy are cultivated while love dies. Once again, our relationships suffer.

Chasing pleasure or running away from pain kills sensitivity, especially spiritual sensitivity. In junior high, we would tell some naive soul, "I'm going to lightly rub the back of your hand with a pencil eraser and you tell me if it starts to hurt." We would gently rub the hand with the eraser but the person would never complain . . . until we stopped! Then they howled and ran around the room, grasping their hand or shaking it in the air while we rolled in laughter. At first, the mind pays attention to the nerve impulses. But long before it starts hurting, the nerve endings become numbed and the mind tunes out the impulses, thinking this is a non-threat. Eventually the skin is broken and, when the rubbing stops, the nerve endings and brain become aware of the pain. It's too late; the damage is done. Similarly, activity to increase pleasure or reduce pain (many of which are good in moderation) slowly lose their potency and require more and more to have the same impact. We lose sensitivity to the effects of these activities until it is too late and some great damage to our lives has been done, usually at the expense of our relationships.

Closing Exercise

Ask God to show you which of these idols you are more likely to pursue. Discuss which idols are most prevalent among your group.

——————— **Day 3** ———————

The *Real* Idol

Ephesians 4:17–24

Yesterday we looked at the three two-faced idols under which all other idols fall. "Two-faced" meaning these idols have two sides, like a coin. To recap, they are:

- seeking security (heads) or escaping insecurity (tails);
- seeking power or control (heads) or escaping commitment, fear, or insignificance (tails); and
- seeking pleasure (heads) or escaping pain or numbness (tails).

Again, idolatry is desiring these things more than we desire God. These idols lead to death of intimacy, love, and spiritual sensitivity. These things ultimately destroy our relationships with others, with ourselves, and with God.

Basically, then, we say, "I want to feel secure, I don't want to feel insecure! I want to have control, I don't want to be trapped! I want to feel good, I don't want to hurt!" What is at the core of all three of these forms of idolatry? Ourselves! They are all about getting what we want. The real idol is the "me god," who demands to be appeased by feeling secure, in control, or satisfied.

This "me god" may sit on the throne of all of our lives or it may only sit on parts of it. Though I had surrendered much of my life to the lordship of Jesus Christ at a fairly young age, I had not yet surrendered my children, my work, or certain aspects of my will. Much of our spiritual journey will involve surrendering the throne of various parts of our lives to Jesus. Sometimes this will be in loving response to what God has done for us, but other times it will be the result of our realizing that the "me god" is making a mess of things and we are on the road to destruction.

However, sometimes when the "me god" steps down, it is something other than Jesus who assumes the throne. More about that later.

Closing Exercise

Ask God to show you an area of your life not yet surrendered to him. Ask him to help you step down from the throne of that part of your life and allow him to assume authority. Share with your group if appropriate and ask them to pray with you about surrendering.

—————— Day 4 ——————
Habitual Sin
Romans 7:21–24; Colossians 3:2–4, 15

God created human beings with an inherent passion to worship and serve. Therefore, we will worship and serve someone or something. This week we have been learning about the "me god," the self that wants to rule its own life. When the "me god" sits on the throne of our lives (or parts of our lives), it screams for security, power, or pleasure, and we respond with behaviors that meet the demand (or at least appear to meet the demand). These behaviors are actually acts of worship to the "me god."

Most of us recognize many of these behaviors as unhealthy and destructive to ourselves and to those around us, but we continue to do them. This is called *habitual sin*.

Habitual because the behaviors have become engrained in us; they are now second nature to us. We do them without thinking because the mind is "set on the flesh/world/self" as Romans 8:5–8 says.

Sin because sin is simply that which separates us from ourselves, others, and God.

Rather than being alert to the presence of the "me god," we focus on the external behaviors. We try to manage these behaviors by pure willpower. But the mind is incapable of choosing something other than what it is set on for more than a short period of time (a year if we're really stubborn and have lots of willpower, about ten minutes if you're like me). Paul says as much in Romans 7.

> I have discovered this principle of life—that when I want to do what is right, I inevitably do what is wrong. I love God's law with all my heart. But there is another power within me that is at war with my mind. This power makes me a slave to the sin that is still within me. Oh, what a miserable person I am! Who will free me from this life that is dominated by sin and death? Thank God! The answer is in Jesus Christ our Lord. . . . (vv. 21–25 NLT)

The solution is not external behavior management and modification, which only exhausts and frustrates us. Rather, the answer is removing the "me god" from the throne of our lives and replacing it with the one true God who has the power to heal our hearts, renew our minds, and transform us. We become changed from the inside out, and changed behavior follows.

Closing Exercise

Continue to ask God to show you if you are convinced of anything that is not true and that is causing you to behave contrary to your beliefs or not fully live in God's truth. If appropriate, share with your group a story from your own life where a false conviction may have formed.

—————— Day 5 ——————
Secondary Idols
Deuteronomy 5:7; Acts 14:11–18; Romans 1:21–23

I want to return to something I previously mentioned. Oftentimes as a person discovers that the "me god" is making a mess of things, the response is to have the "me god" step down. However, rather than having God assume authority, the person puts someone or something else up on the throne.

When people introduce themselves, they often do so either by relational connections or work and accomplishments. This is understandable because we are relational beings who go and do things. It is not surprising that many people set their minds on relationships and put their children, a friend, or a spouse on the throne; and many others set their minds on their work, careers, performance, and accomplishments.

To put something other than God on the throne of our lives is destructive to us and unfair to whatever or whomever we put up there. In the case of another person sitting on the throne, no one except God can properly fill that role. We will resent others for not being enough; they will resent us for expecting them to be our everything, and it's quite possible they will manipulate and take advantage of us. In the case of things being on the throne, all abilities, performance, and careers fade and eventually end. Then what? Gods aren't supposed to fade and die, but all of these false gods will.

One last comment about the need for the "me god" to step down from the thrones of our lives and God to assume his rightful place. This is almost never a once-for-all-time action. It is quite common for us to surrender the throne, only to climb right back on it in the midst of uncertain, fearful, or stressful situations. When that happens, we once again must relinquish the authority to Jesus and trust that he loves us and wants the very best for us.

Closing Exercise

Ask God to show you an area of your life where you may have put someone or something ahead of him, and to help you put him on the throne of that part of your life. Share with your group if appropriate and ask them to pray with you about setting your mind on the things of God first.

Religiosity vs. the Holy Spirit

Day 1

Justifying Grace

Romans 5:1–2, 6–11; 2 Corinthians 5:17;
Ephesians 2:8–9

We will use an illustration throughout this week to help us see how so many church folks become stuck in a powerless, poorly witnessing religiosity. We'll also discover how salvation or being saved is more than what many in our churches understand it to be. Before we jump into the illustration, a word about grace. John Wesley spoke about God's "threefold grace," the first of which I will mention only briefly. *Prevenient grace* is the work of God the Father, through the Holy Spirit, to woo us to himself. Without this pre-grace, we broken sinners would have no hope of finding God and believing in him. More often than not, we only see this work when we look back on our lives and discover how God used people and events (both positive and negative) to open our hearts to his love, truth, and grace.

Let's focus on the second—*justifying grace*—which is offered to us by the Spirit-empowered Son of God through his obedience to the Father. Through Jesus Christ's incarnation, perfect life, sacrificial death, victorious resurrection, glorious ascension, and powerful enthronement over creation, he has made a way for us to be reconciled to God. We receive this grace through faith in Jesus Christ. This is the gospel, the good news of Jesus Christ! Those who are in Christ are positionally righteous, free of sin, and reconciled to the Father. That is to say God only sees the righteousness of Jesus when he interacts with those who are in Christ. There is nothing we have done or could ever do to become righteous like this on our own. Ephesians 2:8 says that it is by grace, through faith, that justification happens and we become new creations.

The third is *sanctifying grace*, which we will discuss tomorrow.

The common problem we human beings face at the justification phase of the salvation process is that we interpret becoming a new creation as becoming a cleaned-up version of the old me who can now live my life basically like I did—except doing a better job at being a good person this time. Maybe two cups of church, a

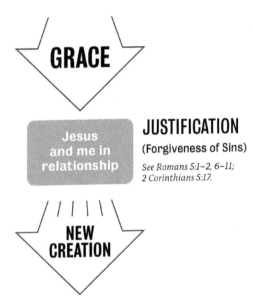

GRACE

JUSTIFICATION
(Forgiveness of Sins)

Jesus and me in relationship

*See Romans 5:1–2, 6–11;
2 Corinthians 5:17.*

NEW CREATION

dash of Bible, and a sprinkle of prayer will help us run our lives better.

What we must understand is that, in the spiritual realm, we are new creations starting out as babies. Like babies, we have little or no idea about what to do next, or how to do it. We are completely helpless and in the arms of Jesus. While we are positionally righteous, we remain functionally fallen human beings living in a broken world. So, what happens next? More on this to come.

Closing Exercise

Share with your group how you have experienced God's prevenient and justifying grace in your life. Ask God to show you things and people in your past that drew you nearer to him. Spend time thanking Jesus for his love, mercy, and saving sacrifice.

—————— **Day 2** ——————

Two Ways to Go

2 Corinthians 5:16–21; Romans 12:1–2; Galatians 3:1–3

Previously we learned about prevenient and justifying grace; how God is always wooing us to himself and how he justified us (made us free of sin and separation from him) through his only Son, Jesus Christ, who came to live among us, teach us, reveal God to us, die in our place to save us from our sin, and rise again to defeat death. We learned that when we put our faith in Jesus, God only sees us through the righteousness of his Son because we are "in Christ."

However, we remain functionally fallen human beings living in a broken world. I am dead to my old self and alive in Christ while still dying to my old self and being raised in Christ. Therefore, what must take place while we live here and now is the ongoing transformation of our hearts, minds, and characters. This second, ongoing work involves God's *sanctifying grace*, which is the transformational work of the Holy Spirit dwelling in us. We are being changed from our broken image into what we were created to be—Christlike people, stamped with the image of God, witnessing to him in the world. This process of sanctification, becoming more and more Christlike, occurs as we cooperate with the Holy Spirit by surrendering or submitting ourselves in obedience to the Holy Spirit. We will talk more about what that looks like, but now I want to share the greatest threat to our sanctification: self-reliance.

Deep within us exists the desire to be in control of our own lives (think "me god"). We think, "I really messed up and need Jesus to clean up my mess." When we accept Jesus' offer of grace and forgiveness, many of us essentially say, "Thanks for the forgiveness, God. I've got it from here." Perhaps we believe that our now-forgiven "me god" is more qualified to sit on the throne, especially if some of the behaviors (acts of worship) the "me god" demands now include religious stuff like Bible reading, praying, serving people, and other religious activities. Quickly these activities drive us toward self-righteousness instead of being means of grace by which we grow in love of God and others.

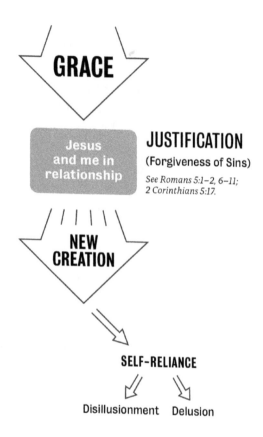

The result is one of two outcomes. The first—disillusionment—comes when we make a mess of our lives again and know it. It produces a defeated, bitter, joyless, jealous Christian who bears no fruit for the kingdom of God. The second—delusion—comes when we think we really are righteous enough to run our own lives. Delusion produces a self-righteous, judgmental, mean-spirited, hard-hearted Christian who bears no fruit for the kingdom of God. Both make poor witnesses and are often cited by nonbelievers as reasons they remain uninterested in faith.

Closing Exercise

Share with your group members if you've ever experienced life down and to the right on the drawing. Describe how that felt (or feels). Also share if you've had cringe-moments (without sharing names) with others who are living in disillusionment or delusion. Ask God to show you if and how you are relying on yourself in your spiritual journey.

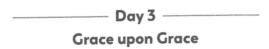

Day 3

Grace upon Grace

Matthew 23:12; John 1:16–18; Romans 5:3–5, 12:1;
James 4:6–11; 1 Peter 5:6–7

The alternative to self-reliance is surrender; to humble oneself under God's mighty right hand. This sounds easy enough, but it is 180 degrees from our nature. What makes it worse is that often when we surrender to the leading of God's Spirit, we are met with difficulty and suffering. It's not that God wants us to be miserable or enjoys causing us pain, rather our broken world hates those surrendered to God (John 15:18–19). The question is not, "Will we suffer if we surrender to God?" but "How will we respond to the suffering we will certainly face?"

Two responses are possible. The first is something like this: "I'm not sure God is doing his job very well. I think I'd better help him out a little bit." This leads us back across the self-reliance path to disillusionment or delusion. The second is perseverance in surrender: obeying,

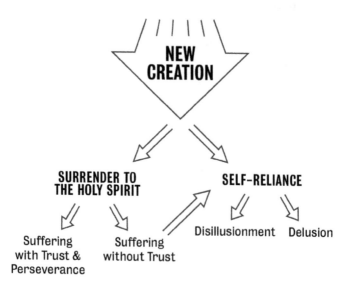

trusting, and learning to hoist on God the inevitable anxieties we will face. I love 1 Peter 5:7 because it tells us that we *will* have anxiety when we humble ourselves under God's authority, but it also tells us that God cares about us, shares in our suffering, and is willing to exchange our anxiety for his peace.

God uses something bad (suffering) to produce something good. What is the good produced? Romans 5:3–5 tells us, "Not only that, but we rejoice in our sufferings, knowing that suffering produces endurance, and endurance produces character, and character produces hope, and hope does not put us to shame, because God's love has been poured into our hearts through the Holy Spirit who has been given to us." Endurance, character, and hope are produced. The other thing it does is it demonstrates the depth of our humility which determines God's timing. (1 Peter 5:6: "at the proper time he may exalt you"). God knows the proper time to lift us up—when we are humble enough to know that we don't deserve to be lifted up and to know that what we need is more grace.

And that's exactly what he does—exalts us upward to receive more grace. This leads to a deeper relationship with him, making us even newer people. And then we get to choose again, and again, and again whether to surrender or to say, "Thanks. I've got it from here." This

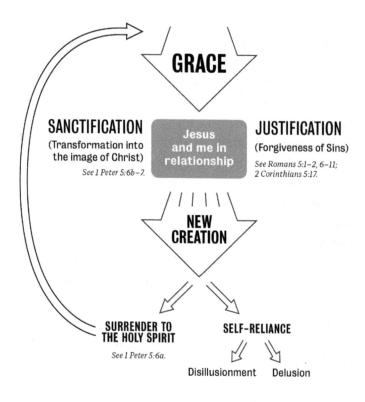

process of surrender, suffering, exaltation, and receiving grace upon grace will continue for the rest of our days, as long as we do not choose down and to the right. This round and round process is called *sanctification*—and sanctification *is* a part of salvation. More on that later.

Closing Exercise

Share with your group a time in your life when you truly surrendered to a leading of God's Spirit. Share how you suffered during that time and how you responded to that suffering.

─────────── **Day 4** ───────────

Salvation Is More than You Think (But Not More than Wesley Thought!)

John 14:23–24; Ephesians 2:8–10; Philippians 2:12–13

I was fortunate to attend a conference where Dallas Willard, nearing the end of his life, spoke about sanctification, discipleship, and spiritual formation. He said that much of the church is preaching something other than the gospel of Jesus Christ. Specifically, it is teaching three types of variant gospel messages that aren't heretical so much as incomplete.

- *The Liberation Gospel.* This message, unfamiliar to the Western evangelical church, focuses on freedom from bondage; not just to sin, but social, political, and systemic bondage. While God clearly opposes oppression of the poor and the marginalized, the gospel of

Jesus Christ is not foremost a message of freedom from societal oppression.

- *The Gospel of How to Be a Good _____ (Baptist, Lutheran, Methodist, Member of This or That Church).* This message begins with Jesus' death and resurrection, but quickly moves down and to the right on our picture because it is all based on works and being right (theologically and morally at best, but at times even racially and politically).

- *The Gospel of How to Get My Ticket Punched to Heaven with Minimal Inconvenience.* The second two are extremely prevalent in the Western church. The results, sad indeed, include stunted spiritual growth in individuals, competition between and even hatred among different churches and denominations, and an unspoken question: What is the least amount I have to do in order to escape hell and slip into heaven?

Justification, having our sins forgiven, is truly amazing and celebrated, but it is not the whole picture of biblical salvation. Saying this will put me in the doghouse with some because we have so focused on getting people into heaven that I'll be accused of a works righteousness viewpoint. But I've already said we can never be righteous enough outside of Christ's imparted righteousness. I'm not saying justification has anything to do with works; I am saying that salvation is not only *justification*, but also *sanctification*. God wants us not only saved from but transformed into; to become who we were meant to be and obediently engaged in his work.

It seems clear to me that this is true when I read the back half of Scriptures like Ephesians 2:8–10. And understanding salvation as justification plus sanctification is the only way one can read Ephesians 2:8–9 ("for it is by grace you have been saved . . . not by works" [NIV]) and Philippians 2:12–13 ("work out your own salvation with fear and trembling") without seeing Paul, the author of both, as being inconsistent or contradictory. We cannot live into God's full salvation and continue forward in our spiritual journey toward Christlikeness without sanctification.

Closing Exercise

Share among your group thoughts you have about the statement: "Salvation is not only justification, but also sanctification," and the question: "Is salvation more than permission to enter heaven?" In light of today's lesson, what does "being saved" mean to you?

———————— **Day 5** ————————

The Three Key Works of the Holy Spirit

Matthew 3:17, 28:18–20; Acts 1:4–5, 8; Romans 8:15–16;
Galatians 5:22–24; 1 Peter 4:8–11

Jesus tells his disciples in Matthew 28, "Go and make disciples of all nations" (v. 19). He also tells them in Acts 1:4, "Do not leave Jerusalem, but wait for the gift my Father promised . . . in a few days you will be baptized with the Holy Spirit." "Go" and "do not leave" are not contradictory here since Jesus tells them that they should stay only until they are empowered by the Holy Spirit, then they should go and be his witnesses. Like the disciples, we receive the Holy Spirit to be powerful witnesses for Jesus. Today I want to share three key works of the Spirit which give us exactly what we need to be good witnesses.

First, the Holy Spirit assures us that we are sons and daughters of God. As Jesus received the Holy Spirit at his baptism, he immediately heard the Father proclaim, "This is my beloved Son, with whom I am well pleased" (Matt. 3:17). As far as we know, Jesus had done nothing in terms of ministry to earn God's pleasure; God was simply pleased to love his Son. We read in Romans 8 that the Holy Spirit speaks to our spirits telling us we are his beloved children (like Jesus at his baptism); the Spirit allows us to call the Creator of the universe *Abba*, or "Daddy." This helps us fully receive God's empowering love.

Second, the Holy Spirit works to change our character as we surrender to him, making us more like Jesus. As our character is transformed, we become empowered to love the Father more. No one loves the Father like the Son, and as we become more and more loving, joyful, peaceful, patient, kind, good, gentle, faithful, and self-controlled, we can love the Father more and more.

Third, the Holy Spirit imparts spiritual gifts to us. There are lists of these gifts in Romans 12, 1 Corinthians 12, and Ephesians 4, but we find the purpose for the spiritual gifts in 1 Corinthians. The end of chapter 12 commands us to eagerly desire these spiritual gifts (v. 31) and the beginning of chapter 14 tells us again to eagerly desire these gifts (v. 1). What chapter is between 12 and 14? Chapter 13, where Paul tells us that we are out to lunch if we desire or use these gifts for anything other than loving people with God's love. These spiritual gifts empower us to do just that, to love others with divine power.

It is amazing that these three key works of the Holy Spirit give us the power necessary to fulfill the Greatest Commandment: to love God and to love others (see Matthew 22:37–38). Next week we will learn how to further cooperate with the Holy Spirit.

Closing Exercise

People sometimes find the Holy Spirit to be a difficult concept because it's easier to grasp God as Father and Jesus as Son, and because peoples' experience of the Holy Spirit can be quite different. Discuss with your group your understanding and experience of the Holy Spirit. Which of the key works mentioned have you most and least experienced?

Cooperation with the Holy Spirit

Day 1

Abide and Obey

John 14:15–21, 15:1–12

In some sense, the entire New Testament outside of the Gospels can be summarized by "abide and obey." We see Jesus doing just that throughout the Gospels, and commanding his followers to do the same going forward. The Epistles are centered around what it means and how it looks to abide and obey. As you read today in John 14 and 15, it is important to note that these two things are intimately linked. For example, "As the Father has loved me, so have I loved you. Abide in my love. If you keep my commandments, you will abide in my love, just as I have kept my Father's commandments and abide in his love" (John 15:9–10 ESV).

Obeying *is* abiding. Abiding *is* obeying. The themes of obedience, God's active presence through his Holy Spirit, complete joy, and real love are all wrapped up together.

As we've learned, one of the key works of the Holy Spirit is transforming each one of us to be more and more like Jesus. Cooperation with the Spirit in this work involves surrendering to God and obeying him as he reveals his will.

> And so, dear brothers and sisters, I plead with you to give your bodies to God because of all he has done for you. Let them be a living and holy sacrifice—the kind he will find acceptable. This is truly the way to worship him. Don't copy the behavior and customs of this world, but let God transform you into a new person by changing the way you think. Then you will learn to know God's will for you, which is good and pleasing and perfect. (Rom. 12:1–2 NLT)

It's submitting to God's will—making his will more important than our will—and then doing what he tells us to do. It's starting what he commands to start, continuing what he tells us to continue, and ending what he desires us to end.

A final thought about abiding and obeying. In our abiding, we need to be aware of God's grace to us in our failures to obey. It is so easy for us to slip into a human-centered religious perspective that makes obeying the prerequisite for God being present with us in love. God pursued us and Jesus died for us while we were sinners; his love is not earned by our obedience.

Closing Exercise

Review your calendar over the past two weeks or start today and review each day forward for two weeks. Take note of the time you spend abiding in God—spending time focused on him and his presence in your life. Also look for time munchers—activities that produce no fruit in terms of loving God, loving others, serving God, or serving others. Ask God to renew your mind about these activities and try to create space to abide more in God as you eliminate fruitless activity.

--------- **Day 2** ---------

Thanksgiving and Service

Mark 9:35; 2 Corinthians 4:5; Galatians 5:13;
Philippians 4:6; 1 Thessalonians 5:16–18

I am a second, possibly third, career pastor. I felt called to ministry from a very early age, but when it was time to commit to that call, I ran like Jonah! I became a chemical engineer and worked for 3M for seven years (Scotch tape, Command strips . . . you know them). Then

I worked alongside my lifelong friend in his family business as the general manager. During that time, God did some amazing work in my life and then brought the call back around to me. I had a family and a mortgage, so I began attending Asbury Theological Seminary while still working, taking advantage of their extended learning program online and their July/January intensive terms. A local church hired me as their discipleship pastor while I was still working through the slow one-class-at-a-time process. While I wouldn't recommend it as the best way to get one's master of divinity, it did have its advantages. I want to highlight two of them.

The first is that I could immediately apply what I was learning and what God was doing in me to my work in the church. The second is a bit harder to explain. I have many friends who say that their sequestered time in seminary was rich in community and fertile ground to prepare for ministry. However, they also said they had difficulty after graduation because they were never going to find the environment in which they had spent the last three to four years, an environment that was in some ways very focused on them.

That's a long introduction to make this important point. The spiritual formation process can become self-absorbed and inwardly focused because it involves asking

God to show us where we need to grow in knowledge, faith, love, forgiveness, etcetera. Preventing the process from becoming solely about us requires a two-ingredient antidote—*gratitude* and *service to others*.

Being grateful in every situation, in the midst of mountaintop or desert circumstances, helps us keep a long-term and God-centered perspective on our lives and spiritual growth. Serving others regularly in tangible ways, with no expectation of reward or recognition, allows us to immediately apply what God is doing in us. It helps us remember that we love and serve him when we love and serve others. We are growing, maturing, and becoming more like Christ for his purposes in the world and the people around us, not for ourselves.

Abiding, obeying, giving thanks, and serving are ways we cooperate with God's Spirit as he transforms us more and more into the image of Christ.

Closing Exercise

Share with your group members which of the two—giving thanks or serving others—is more natural for you. Challenge yourself and one another to give thanks each day for what God is doing in your life (even the hard things), and to find a way to serve someone in the next week in a practical way with kindness.

Day 3

God Is the Best Jenga Player Ever!

Psalm 51:10–12; 139:1–18, 23–24;
Romans 8:26–28; 1 John 3:19–20

When we accept Jesus, receive his grace, and surrender to the Holy Spirit, we become more aware of our sin and disobedience. This is because the Spirit convicts us of our sin (John 16:7–13; 2 Corinthians 7:9–10). This type of conviction, this sense of guilt, is not a bad thing; rather it is God being a good Father to us, to let us know we've messed up so we can repent and receive his gracious forgiveness through Jesus Christ. Condemnation = bad, the work of Satan; Conviction = good, the work of the Holy Spirit.

As we learned the second week of our study, we need to know the full extent of the IOU in order to forgive. The same is true in reverse; we need to get a grasp on our own IOU in order to fully receive God's forgiveness. The Spirit helps us realize our IOU, repent, receive forgiveness, and then work to remove that area of sin from our lives. Here, many well-meaning church folks can get in the way of God's transformational work in a person's life by deputizing themselves as junior holy spirits and convicting people of their sin (judging the person, not the sin). They decide which sins are most egregious and therefore must be dealt with first, and then demand that the person clean up their act if they are to be loved, drawn closer to Christ, and discipled. The result is people feeling condemned and further distanced from God. Sometimes we do this to ourselves, choosing the sin we hate worst and wanting to change it first, then trying to do so in our own power. Good luck! There's a reason that the first step in a twelve-step program is admitting you can't solve your problem or change on your own.

The Holy Spirit, on the other hand, is the best Jenga player ever. I hope you know the game Jenga. It's played with a stack of wooden pieces laid three across in rows, one on top of the other in alternating directions. Players take turns pulling a piece from the stack and replacing it on top. The game ends when someone knocks the tower over. Jenga is a good metaphor for our lives, though you need to imagine a tower with wooden pieces of different sizes and shapes, some with red Xs. We want to pull out the biggest block with the most obvious red X on it. But our efforts to do so only collapse the tower. Lives crumble under the weight and pressure of trying to remove that piece from the tower.

Of course, we can't pretend like there are no red Xs in our lives, but neither can we try to sanctify ourselves or surrender authority for the process to the more judgmental folks in our churches. Instead, we need to allow the Spirit, who knows exactly which blocks to pull, lead us in the lifelong Jenga game that is our spiritual journey toward sanctification.

Closing Exercise

Ask God to reveal to you what area of your life he wants to work on with you next. Also ask him to reveal any relationship in which you are trying to play the role of the Holy Spirit in someone's life rather than support what the Spirit is already doing with that person.

––––––––––––– **Day 4** –––––––––––––

The Holy Spirit and Chocolate Milk

Acts 2:1–4, 22–24, 36–39; 4:23–31; Ephesians 5:18

Imagine a glass of milk, white and liquid. Now imagine a copious amount of delicious, Hershey's chocolate syrup being poured into the milk. Is it chocolate milk now? If you took a drink would it taste different than white milk? No and no. It's only white milk with chocolate in the bottom. The chocolate needs to be stirred up in order to transform it into chocolate milk. If we put that chocolate milk in the fridge for a couple of days, it will again become milk with chocolate in it.

The glass of milk represents a life, and the chocolate is the Holy Spirit. The milk may receive the chocolate, but nothing changes until it is stirred up. Just like the difference between milk with chocolate in it and chocolate milk, there is a difference between a life with the Holy Spirit's presence and a Spirit-filled life. In Acts 2, Peter gives the normative way the Holy Spirit is received: repent, believe, receive forgiveness, and be baptized. The rest of the first half of Acts seems to tell the story of exceptions to that norm. People did what Peter said, yet appeared to receive the Holy Spirit later, only after someone prayed with them. I believe these accounts actually describe people who received the Holy Spirit but needed stirring.

The account in Acts 4 says that the disciples who had been filled with the Holy Spirit on Pentecost were "filled" again (v. 31). I believe they experienced a fresh stirring of the Spirit as a result of their praying together. A proper translation of Ephesians 5:18 is "keep on being filled with the Holy Spirit again and again." Or said another way, "keep having the Spirit stirred up in you again and again." What stirs up the Spirit in our lives? Spiritual disciplines (or means of grace)—prayer, reading the Bible, corporate worship, and the Lord's Supper. Clearly the Bible says having others pray for us is a strong stirring force. But there are others, perhaps more unique to individuals, like walking in nature, spiritual conversations with good friends, and mentoring or being mentored by others. We all have our spiritual spoons that better stir us up.

Two things to consider or remember about being stirred up. First, as you grow spiritually, it is common that the things that stir up the Spirit in you change. Don't become so comfortable with certain practices that you miss the change and stunt your growth. Second, we are stirred up not for some spiritual, experiential high, but to serve God effectively as witnesses and ambassadors, just like the disciples in Acts 4 who, afterward, went out and preached boldly.

Closing Exercise

Share with your group how "chocolate" your life looks currently. Ask God to show you what might be helpful in stirring the Spirit up in you this next season of life. Ask your group members or trusted family members and friends if they see patterns in your life that result in "white milk" living.

—————— Day 5 ——————
Healing in Community
Genesis 2:18; John 21:10–17; Galatians 6:1–2;
1 Thessalonians 5:14–15

This is our last day together, so I want to summarize what we have learned and add an important component of cooperation with the Spirit to move forward in your spiritual journey. In the first week, we asked the four big questions of spiritual formation.

- Where am I? (Unique to each individual. Location is less important than being pointed in the right direction!)

- Where am I going? (As Christians, we are going on to Christlikeness; reflecting more and more the image of Christ to the world. Over time, this means I become more loving, joyful, peaceful, patient, kind, good, gentle, faithful, and self-controlled.)

- Do I *want* to go there or only wish I was more Christlike? (Wanting to go means I'm willing to do and endure hard things to get there.)

- What are the obstacles keeping me from getting there? (We mentioned three common ones; unfor-giveness, living out of lies deep in our hearts, and idols—particularly the "me god" who sits on the throne when we try to control our own lives.)

Recall the less-than-flattering image I used for a stuck spiritual journey: a dog hooked to a long leash, tethered to a post in the ground. There are times when the post is shallow or the leash is weak, so the dog pulling harder gets him free to run forward again. Other times the post is deep and the leash is strong, so that no amount of running harder will move the dog forward; it only exhausts him. Likewise, when we are spiritually stuck, there are times when reading our Bible more, praying more, and so on, will break us free. But there are other times where we will only exhaust ourselves with more spiritual activity.

This is when we need a healthy spiritual community to help us remove whatever obstacle has us bound. Forgiving someone who wounded us deeply, discovering lies that reside deep in our hearts, healing from the wounds or pride that gave birth to those lies, and learning to surrender our lives and trust God more than we trust ourselves all require the help of others.

In all of God's creation before the fall, there was one thing not yet good: that Adam was alone. And in the aftermath of Peter's shameful abandonment of Jesus at his most difficult hour, Jesus chose to restore him relationally and authoritatively after a meal and in front of all of his other friends and ministry partners. We were made for community and relationship, we are wounded and fall in community and relationship, and we will be healed and restored in community and relationship. There is no better reason to be a part of a local church, a small group where the relationships grow to be authentic and deep, and to find good spiritual direction and sound counseling. While it is Jesus who heals, he does so in the context of community.